Cross-Cultural ECE

Cross-Cultural Role Plays, Case Studies, and Job Simulations

Dave Cornell, Ph.D.

Copyright © 2019 by David P. Cornell

All rights reserved. No part of this publication may be reproduced, distributed, or transmitted in any form or by any means, including photocopying, recording, or other electronic or mechanical methods, without the prior written permission of the author, except in the case of brief quotations embodied in critical reviews and certain other noncommercial uses permitted by copyright law. For permission requests, contact Dr. Cornell at: dcornell33304@yahoo.com

ISBN: 978-0-578-52726-0

DEDICATION

This book is dedicated to my mother and father, Patricia and Dewey. "A mother's job is never done," was my mother's driving force. "Life is tough all over," words of wisdom from my father. May they both rest in peace.

ACKNOWLEDGMENTS

Writing a book takes a lot of time and is usually the result of getting help from other people along the way. The situation with this book is a little different. There is not a graphic artist or a copy editor, or any of the team members associated with traditional publishing. There are basically an author and people that tolerated their obsession. In this case, the "people" is named Cindy. Cindy has been a part of this book's development from the very beginning. She has listened to me explain the scenarios over many years and given her opinion about which ones I should include or leave out. That advice has been exceptionally helpful. The first draft of this book was well over 200 pages. Two-hundred pages would have been far too many.

Cindy also has a very wise and diplomatic perspective. She was quick to point out which scenarios were a little too harsh and offensive to an Eastern culture, and since the purpose of the book is not to offend, that advice was taken. So, thank you Cindy, for your patience and wisdom, and natural sense of diplomacy.

FOREWORD

The main purpose of this book is to provide future educators with valuable insights into cross-cultural issues they will likely encounter while working in a foreign country as a teacher or principal. While nothing beats direct experience, reading about and discussing cross-cultural issues in the safety of a classroom environment can better prepare those interested in making the ambitious leap to working abroad. All case studies and role-plays presented in this book are true events encountered by the author while working in Asia for 12 years. With that said, nearly all of the scenarios described are based on actual events in one country in particular. I have thought long and hard about whether to identify that country by name. Ultimately, I chose not to reveal the name of that country, for a variety of reasons.

Readers might also notice that the book is only about what happens in the classroom. Of course, working in a foreign country also involves encountering different cultural practices in social situations. Table etiquette and social customs have been intentionally excluded. There is no need to call attention to cultural habits that Westerners might find repellent. My objective is not to disparage anyone's culture or embarrass people in another country.

With that said, working in a foreign country is not always a bed of roses. Being the only foreigner in a room full of people with a strong sense of nationalism and skewed concept of fairness can be a truly terrible experience. The role-plays throughout the book are designed to make students feel what it is like to have everyone at the table working against you.

The differences between classroom practices in the West and East are substantial. The book's cover image symbolizes the situation; like two cars going in opposite directions. The predominant way of thinking, and very often stated out loud, is "this is _____", and therefore, everything should be done the _____ way. You can insert the name of several countries in that blank. To be fair, you can probably insert the name "United States" if this book were about foreign teachers working in the U.S.

When a principal or teacher from an Eastern educational system sees a kindergarten classroom with kids laughing and being loud (due to their enthusiasm), it must be like fingernails on a chalkboard (apologies for the outdated metaphor). They simply cannot stand it, and they will take steps to stop it immediately; even to the point of walking into the classroom and yelling at the kids to "be quiet." This has happened to nearly every foreign teacher I have spoken to in one particular country, and it happened to me on numerous occasions.

The irony of this situation cannot be overstated. On the one hand, the local parents want their children to be expressive and become great innovators and creators. A photo of Steve Jobs can be found in schools everywhere. This is why parents pay so much extra tuition for an international school, or for a bilingual school that has a Western teacher in the classroom all day. But yet, the education system in some Eastern countries prohibits free-thinking. Classroom practices are teacher-centered and focused on rote memorization. Students learn at an early age that their role is to sit quietly and listen to the teacher. Asking questions is seen as confrontational and disrespectful of the teacher's authority. And yet, at the same time, the list of local schools trying to obtain IB certification (known for the inquiry method of teaching), is staggering. The people at IB don't have enough personnel to handle the demand.

Aside from what happens in the classroom, there are other unpleasantries for foreign teachers that make life difficult. It's not just a deep pedagogical divide that exists between two contrasting philosophies. The frequency with which a foreign teacher is treated rudely and unprofessionally is astounding. It is pervasive. The case studies presented throughout this book are really just the tip of the iceberg. Many examples that I could have included were not, for the simple reason that they were just too extreme. My objective is not to embarrass or point the finger at any one particular country, but to provide prospective foreign teachers with insights about how they might be treated.

As you read the case studies and scenarios, you could easily conclude that this sort of thing could happen in any country, East or West. That is absolutely true. But in one country in particular, there is a level of pervasiveness that will not be seen elsewhere. The crassness aimed at foreign teachers occurs on a daily basis. It is not something that just happens occasionally, to just an unfortunate few. Moreover, if there is ever a disagreement between a foreign teacher and a local one, the management team will always, and I mean always, take the side of the local teacher.

So, my hope for this book is to turn something negative into something positive. University students can explore how to handle cross-cultural conflicts in the safety of the classroom. They can benefit from discussing conflict resolution strategies with other students and receiving advice from their professor.

With that said, I also hope that the content does not offend people in Eastern countries. There are many great teachers in Asia and many of them have adopted a more Western approach. No one likes to have their country portrayed in a negative light. For this reason, I included several scenarios that also involve foreign teachers and administrators being difficult and unreasonable, in an attempt to be more balanced. I hope users of the book will benefit and grow as aspiring professionals so that we can all do a better job achieving what we all really want: educating children.

HOW TO USE THIS BOOK

This course supplement contains five types of small group activities: Case Studies that involve small group discussion, Role Plays, Action Plan Job Simulations, YouTube videos that include small group activities, and an On-the-Spot card game. In addition, there are Self-reflection worksheets and Research Investigation worksheets for additional learning dynamics. Each are described below.

Case Studies:
The main component of the book involves a written description of a true scenario encountered by the author. The course instructor can use the scenario as part of a small group activity or class discussion. Each scenario has 10 discussion points. Feel free to use all or only some of those.

When used as a small group activity, each group can discuss each point and then share their experience with the rest of the class. This can lead to other groups offering feedback or commentary that may be helpful to understanding the cross-cultural dynamics involved in the scenario.

YouTube Videos:
To liven up the classroom, this book also has links to several short videos on YouTube that portray the case studies or other cross-cultural scenarios. The instructor can simply play one of the short videos in class, then have the students discuss the issues presented at the end of the video. Links and QR codes are placed at various spots throughout the book.

Research Investigations:
Some case studies also include an opportunity for students to research an issue in more detail by gathering factual information regarding the scenario. This worksheet is provided in the book at designated places. This will help students gain experience finding research-based information and obtain practice using proper APA referencing.

Action Plans:
Working in a school often means encountering serious issues and trying to generate effective solutions in collaboration with others. In a cross-cultural context, this can become more complicated. Knowing how to make and use an Action Plan is a valuable way to approach situations in an organized and systematic manner. So, some Case Studies include an Action Plan activity for groups to use either as an in-class or out of class assignment. Each Action Plan form is located at the end of the Case Study.

Role-Plays:
Many of the Case Studies lend themselves to role-plays. After reading the scenario, students

engage in a role play regarding that situation. Each role comes with a brief description of that person's character and main concerns. Students can gain valuable practice negotiating conflict and competing demands in the safety of a classroom setting, guided by their instructor's sage advice.

To make this activity more beneficial, one person in the group can play the role of Observer. The Observer uses the Team Meeting Assessment Scale to assess the group dynamics of how the members interact with each other. The Observer then provides feedback to the group as a whole, which will enable individual members to better understand how their actions affect the group. The Scale is located in the Appendix.

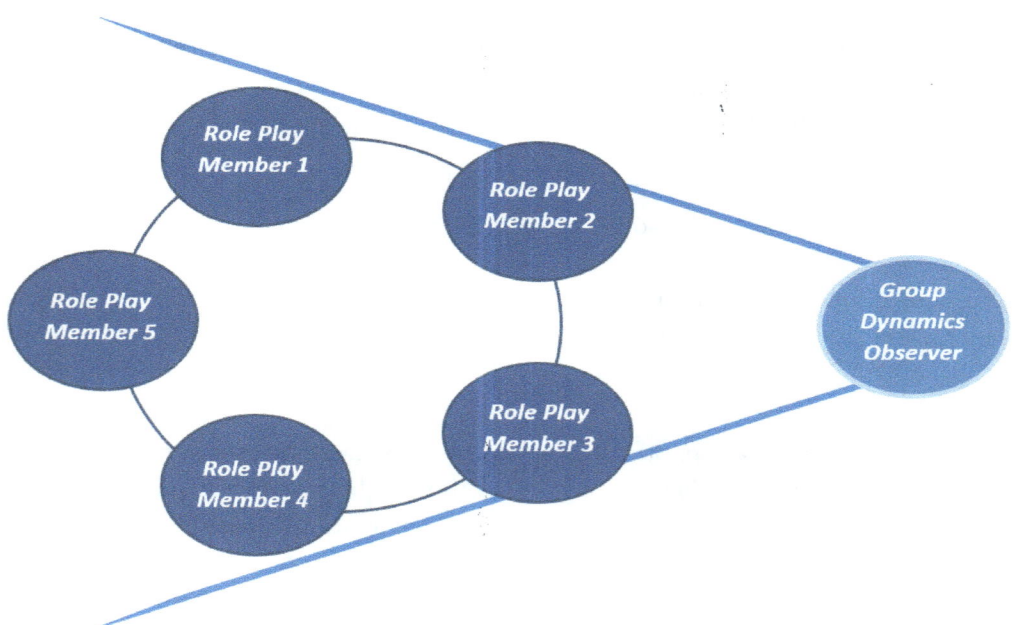

On-the-Spot Card Game:
This is a fast-paced card game that involves each player giving their opinion on how to handle a specific scenario. First, form small groups of 3-5 players. Cut out the cards on one of the pages and place them in a stack in the center of the group. One player then picks the top card and reads aloud the scenario described. Then that player says how they would respond and what they would say in that situation. Afterwards, the other members of the group share their opinions on the player's response and how they would handle it.

A slightly different version of this game involves the group discussing the scenario and then arriving at a consensus on what to say and do. It is important to be as specific as possible. So, instead of saying something in general, try to write down the specific words that your group thinks should be used in that scenario. Finally, each group can share their solution with the class and the course instructor can guide a class discussion.

Note: One aspect of conflict resolution is knowing when the situation is serious and when it is best to just "let it go." Not all of the scenarios described on the cards are extremely serious. It is the students that must determine when the situation merits confrontation, or diplomacy, or just seeing the matter as frivolous and not worth a long and possibly heated discussion.

Self-reflection:
Self-reflection worksheets give students an opportunity to think about their actions and feelings after the role-plays and job simulations. Students can identify ways they would like to improve and make adjustments to how they collaborate with others in the future. This worksheet is located in the Appendix.

Table of Contents

You are the Foreign Teacher 1
- Questioning Authority 2
- YouTube: Questioning Authority 4
- Teacher Shunning Student 5
- Salary and Accommodations 7
- Oh, by the way… 9
- Be quiet! 11
- YouTube: Be Quiet 13
- The Test-Switcheroo Trick 14
- Not My Job... 17
- Balance Beam Action Plan 20
- YouTube: On the Edge of Their Seats 23
- YouTube: Finger in Face 24

You are the Foreign Principal 25
- Hand-foot-and mouth Disease Action Plan 26
- Outdoor Playground Safety Plan 30
- Christmas Show Sabotage 33
- Pocket Knife in the Kindy 37
- Trampoline Fun 39
- YouTube: Trampoline Trouble 41
- Double Trouble 43
- Termination Letter 45
- YouTube: Four Against One 47
- YouTube: Applicant Requirements 41
- YouTube: Division of Labor 49

On the Spot 50
- Appendix A: Self-Reflection Worksheet 60
- Appendix B: Setting New Goals Worksheet 62
- Appendix C: Observer Form 63
- About the Author 64

You are the Foreign Teacher

1 Questioning Authority

Setting the Scene:

Teachers' meetings are frequent at your new school. The local principal often explains new rules or changes in policies handed down from the school's owner. There are cautionary statements regarding classroom management, announcements about future school events and activities, and always a few notes regarding parental complaints. You have noticed that there is very little, actually no discussion. The principal talks and everyone else listens. The local teachers seem to be taking notes diligently and nod in agreement throughout. Your foreign colleagues sit attentively, but never ask a question about anything.

During one meeting, a policy about nap-time is explained that seems counter-intuitive to you, and even a little contradictory from rules that were given a few weeks prior. So, you raise your hand and point-out that what is being explained now is different from what was stated previously. You immediately sense a chill in the room. The principal is quiet for several seconds and then states that the new policy should be followed, as was just stated. Because you think that the previous policy was better for the kids, you give a couple of reasons why you think the older rules were best. The principal repeats, almost verbatim, what she said in response to your first comment.

After the meeting is finished everyone returns to the teachers' office. But, on the way, a few of the foreign teachers stop you and one of them tells you that what you did was "wrong." He explains that in this country, teachers do not question or disagree with the principal, especially in a meeting. Another teacher chimes-in and agrees, stating that you "embarrassed" the principal by pointing out a discrepancy in the policy and then made it worse by giving reasons why the new policy is wrong. The culture of this country is very hierarchical and status oriented. Even asking a question can be seen as disrespecting the principal's authority. You try to defend yourself by saying that you were just expressing your opinion about a rule you thought was not in the students' best interest. At that point, a third foreign teacher, who has been in the country for several years, says, "You are in their country, so you need to respect their ways. We are guests here."

Discuss the questions below from your own perspective in small groups of 3-5 members.

1) What is your initial reaction to this situation?

2) Do you think asking the principal a question is being confrontational?

3) Do you think that disagreeing with the principal, after she restated the policy, is

questioning her authority in front of others?

4) Is there a better way for the teacher in the meeting to have handled her concerns?

5) Many people in this region of the world have a deep resentment of colonialism. Western foreigners are often seen as condescending and arrogant. Can you understand how this may make disagreeing with a local person in a position of authority reinforce this view?

6) If you were the local principal, would you feel as though your authority is being questioned?

7) If the meeting was in your home country and a foreign teacher acted the same way, would the principal be offended?

8) What is your opinion regarding: "You are in their country, so you need to respect their ways."

9) Does living in a foreign country mean giving up your right to express an opposing opinion?

10) Do you think the foreign teacher should approach the local principal and offer an apology?

YouTube Video Supplement

Instructions:

The video on YouTube is a reenactment of this scenario which can be used for a class discussion. The course instructor can play the video in class and guide a class discussion, or create several small groups to engage in their own discussions. If in small groups, then each group should try to reach a consensus on how the matter should be handled. When each group has formulated a resolution, they can take turns sharing their solution with the class.

Questioning Authority:
https://www.youtube.com/watch?v=fT4dvK0Pdo4&t=35s
Copy and paste the URL or scan the QR code:

2 Teacher Shunning Student

Setting the Scene:

You have been in the country for several months. One thing you learned about regional history is that there is a great deal of resentment towards Japan. The Japanese military committed atrocities during WWII on several Asian countries, and many people in Southeast Asia have not forgotten.

One day another class is joining yours for a holiday activity. Teachers have prepared arts and crafts at different tables. Students spend 20 minutes at each table and then move on. Of course, one table is getting the most interest. As one Japanese boy in your class tries to get a better look at an already crowded table, the local teacher gently, but firmly nudges him away and says "No" in a stern tone. The boy is not easily deterred and tries again. The fourth time, the teacher grabs the student by his arm and pulls him away from the table. The boy finally gives up and goes to another table.

Discuss the questions below from your own perspective in small groups of 3-5 members.

1) What reason do you think the teacher has for preventing the student from joining the group?

2) Could she have used a different tactic?

3) Do you think the different nationalities and history involved played a role?

4) Should you have intervened?

5) Should you report this incident to the foreign or local principal, or write about it in the diary for the Japanese boy's parents to read?

6) What kind of learning environment is being created for the student?

7) If you were the principal and saw this, how would you respond?

8) If you were this boy's parent and saw this, how would you respond?

9) Is there a difference between a foreign and local teacher's responsibility to handle this situation?

10) Should the school have a policy regarding this situation?

Role-Play Instructions:

The boy's mother happened to see this act on the school's CCTV web-stream and has asked to have a meeting with the principal. So, a meeting is called to discuss the matter. Run this simulation with just four players: the mother, the two principals, and one passive Observer.

Cut out the cards below and place in a stack face down in the center of the table. Each person takes a card at the top of the stack. Read the characteristics of your role, then act accordingly during the meeting. Try to genuinely represent that person's point of view. When the meeting has finished, the Observer can provide feedback and advice on how the meeting transpired and how it might be improved if the meeting were to occur again.

The Objective: Come to a consensus regarding this matter and how it should be handled in the future.

Foreign Principal	**Local Principal**
Is aware of the deep resentment of what happened in WWII	Feels obligated to protect and defend the local teacher
Is aware of similar actions towards Japanese students in this country	Persistently tries to say the teacher's actions were not unprofessional or culturally motivated
Has to strike a balance between protecting the school's reputation and responding to the parent's concerns	Has ancestors that were victims of Japanese atrocities during WWII

Japanese Parent	**Observer**
Witnessed the pushing on CCTV	Trained professional observer
Has no option to leave the school	Expert in group dynamics, leadership and conflict resolution
Is very protective of only child	
Wary of the local teacher's motives	Provides feedback and advice at end of meeting
Too polite to show strong emotion or be confrontational, but wants a resolution	

3 Salary and Accommodations

Setting the Scene:

After finishing your contract in a foreign country and spending the summer back home in the USA, you start searching for another position. After many months and a few online interviews, you eventually land a great position as the Foreign Director of an IB (International Baccalaureate) kindergarten. Being Director is very exciting, and from the looks of the school's website, the school is well-equipped. It turns out that the kindergarten is part of a much larger boarding school that includes a primary and secondary school as well. The students all go home for the weekends and most of them live in a city several hours away where school tuitions are much higher.

The boarding school has over 5,000 students, and the campus is complete with multiple swimming pools (indoor and out), tennis courts, volleyball and basketball courts everywhere, as well as a large library and numerous computer rooms. All the classrooms have interactive white boards and teachers are expected to dress professionally and conduct all classes with high standards.

According to the contract, the salary for the job is very good and the school also provides a free apartment. You sign the contract and send it to the HR department. They explain that all you have to do is arrive on a business visa, which they will help with, and then all of the government regulations for obtaining a work visa will be handled once you arrive.

So, you agree and are looking forward to learning about the country's traditional teaching philosophy. Your first two days will involve IB training, which you are also looking forward to. After agreeing to terms with the school, you embark on this exciting journey.

A few weeks later, you have just arrived at the airport, which you were told "is near" the school. After 32 hours, 4 planes, and 12 time zones, you can only think of 2 things: showering and sleep. But your trip is not over. Once you land at the airport and go through immigration and customs, you then take a bus to another location about 30-minutes away and wait for someone from the school to pick you up in a van. The van shows-up 30 minutes late and approximately 90 minutes later you arrive at the school.

When the HR assistant shows you to your apartment, supplied by the school, you enter and see: a coffee table with a cracked glass top held together with tape; a sofa with its vinyl torn in several places exposing the cushions; wooden chest of drawers with no handles; pencil and marker scribblings on several walls; chipped paint; and accumulated dirt and grime in the corners, baseboards and floors. For the final icing on the cake, in the bathroom you see 3 large, dead, roach-like insects lying on the shower floor. You're not sure what kind of insects they are, but they are large, and dead. Unfortunately, you are already 2 hours late for the first day of IB training, currently in progress. You tell the assistant that you would like to take a shower, but when you point to the dead insects in the shower, she seems unfazed.

Discuss the questions below from your own perspective in small groups of 3-5 members.

1) The assistant says there is no other shower, so the question becomes "to shower, or not to shower?

2) When you get to the IB training room, the kindergarten's local director greets you and says abruptly "You're late". What is your response?

3) The local principal greets you and asks warmly "how are you?" Your response?

4) Do you think that expressing a "concern" at that moment about the room will be too soon?

5) Americans have a reputation in this part of the world as being big complainers and too direct. Important here?

6) That night you sleep on a hard bed, no sheets, one blanket and a pillow. How do you feel the next morning before another full day of training?

7) The local principal greets you again and asks, "how did you sleep?" Your response?

8) A parent is there and says, "is everything okay? you look tired."

9) When and with whom would you discuss the accommodation issue? Or would you?

10) Americans have a very strict definition of *clean* compared to many other cultures. Can you accept this cultural difference regarding the concept of clean?

4 Oh, by the way…

Setting the Scene:

This scenario is a continuation of the previous one. At the end of that day's IB training, the head of school informs you that you cannot be the foreign director because you cannot speak the local language. She then asks if you would not mind being the grade level coordinator and teacher of a K2 class instead. You are assured that there will be no change in your salary or accommodation. Of course, saying "no" means being stranded in a foreign country with no family or friends, and no job. So, you agree. After all, you can still learn a lot about the culture and the school has a very good reputation.

The next morning during the coffee break of the IB training, the principal of the kindergarten informs you that you cannot be the grade level coordinator because they already have someone in that position and she is upset about being replaced. Surely you understand how she feels. The principal explains that you will be the lead teacher in the K2 classroom. You agree.

After the second day of IB training has finished, the director of the kindergarten greets you and then states, in a very matter-of-fact tone, that you cannot be the lead teacher in the classroom. The lead teacher must be able to speak the local language fluently so they can communicate with the parents. You can be a foreign homeroom teacher. He explains that the previous foreign teacher had to be let go a few weeks ago because they showed a "bad working attitude". The parents are, understandably, really upset. They pay a higher tuition to ensure there is a native English-speaking teacher in the classroom all day. He says the school has been looking for a replacement and of course, there will be no change in your salary or accommodation.

Discuss the questions below from your own perspective in small groups of 3-5 members.

1) How are you feeling at this point?

2) Would you accept this final demotion and agree to be the foreign teacher in the K2 classroom?

3) If you refused, what would you do next?

4) The parents are upset there is not a native English-speaking foreign teacher in the classroom, can you understand the school's predicament?

5) When you suggest working half time as a teacher and half time as director, the school

does not agree. Would you still accept the position as foreign teacher?

6) Would you consider seeking legal advice?

7) What advice would you give yourself about how to avoid this situation in the future?

8) After working at the school for a few months and speaking with other foreign teachers, you discover that there are other instances of contractual terms being changed. What kind of work environment do you think this creates?

9) Despite all the challenges, you really like the kids, and the salary, so is it really such a bad deal?

10) At the end of the school year, you're offered a 2-year contract as a classroom foreign teacher.
Do you accept?

Small Group Activity:
Form small groups of 3-5 members and work through the activity in the box below.

> First, working alone, list the different events in this scenario, if any, that would upset you.
>
> _____
>
> _____
>
> Second, discuss your list with the other members of your group.
>
> Third, choose 1 event and form a group consensus on exactly what to say and who to say it to at that moment.
>
> _____
>
> _____

5 Be Quiet!

Setting the Scene:

The director of the kindergarten has asked you to teach extra classes. He compliments your teaching style and how enthusiastic the students become during your classes. You accept under the condition that you can use the materials and methods that you want. The director agrees.

In your judgment, the kids need to have a little fun in class, especially given the very controlling manner of the local teachers. They demand that the kids sit still and quietly at all times. The usual form of instruction is that the students listen and repeat what the teacher says. Everything is highly restrictive and controlled. If a student begins to express some excitement or release some pent-up energy, they are immediately scolded. This is the teaching style that is predominant throughout the country; every morning class, every afternoon class, every day. So, for 30 minutes, twice a week, they get to have fun when their foreign teacher arrives for English class. The kids love the lessons and they actually learn as well (a little...after all, it's only 30 minutes twice a week).

One day you are teaching a lesson about transportation. In part of the lesson, you say the name of the vehicle, use it in a sentence, then make a silly noise and action that matches that particular vehicle. In the beginning, the kids repeat, then later they do it by themselves. The kids love the activity, especially the part where they get to make a silly noise and action. As children ages 4-5 years old can sometimes, they get a little loud, but you manage to calm them down and then move on to the next vehicle on the list for that day. At one point during the lesson, when the kids are a bit loud, again, the local teacher from next door enters your classroom, walks directly up to the students, and with hands on hips, tells them quite sternly to "be quiet" (in their native language). All of the kids immediately stop and sit down.

Discuss the questions below from your own perspective in small groups of 3-5 members.

1) What is your first reaction to this scenario?

2) Can you understand the local teacher's perspective?

3) If you were the local teacher and you did not like the loudness of the class, how would you have handled the situation?

4) Is it acceptable for one teacher to address the students of another teacher during their class?

5) Can you think of situations in which it would be acceptable for one teacher to address the students of another teacher?

6) What would you do if this happened to you?

7) If you were the principal and happened to see this entire scenario, how would you handle it?

8) Should the foreign teacher modify their teaching style to fit the local culture and teaching philosophy?

9) Should the local teacher modify their expectations and accept the Western teacher's philosophy?

10) Should the school have a policy regarding this scenario?

Instructions:

Staying in the same group as with the discussion activity above, now play the role of school administrators and write a policy regarding this issue. Make sure to clearly discuss your working concepts and design a policy that shows fair consideration of cultural differences.

Group Objective:
Write a school policy statement regarding co-teachers having different instructional and classroom management practices in the classroom.

YouTube Video Supplement

Instructions:

The video on YouTube is a reenactment of this scenario which can be used for a class discussion. The course instructor can play the video in class and guide a class discussion or create several small groups to engage in a discussion. Each group should try to reach a consensus on how the matter should be handled. When each group has formulated a resolution, they can take turns sharing their solution with the class.

Be Quiet:
https://www.youtube.com/watch?v=DSSf7vAgg7I
Copy and paste the URL or scan the QR code:

6 The Test-Switcheroo Trick

Setting the Scene:

You are working in a newly established international division of a local primary school. The team consists of 2 local directors, 5 local teachers and 2 foreign teachers. You are one of the foreign teachers. Although you are in a teaching role, you were hired due to your previous experience helping businessmen and women open kindergartens, which you have accomplished on several occasions so far. The school plans to open a new kindergarten on campus the following year, and you are to step into a management role when that occurs.

You and the other foreign teacher have completely different philosophies about working in a foreign country. He passively accepts the rules and instructions of the local management team. At meetings he doesn't ask any questions and always nods in agreement.

However, in your opinion, the rules are too restrictive and similar to local schools. The international division is supposed to be "international." The parents pay extra for their child to experience Western teaching practices. Sometimes you ask questions at meetings and express disagreement with some of the stated policies and instructions. This approach offends the local directors because questioning leadership is interpreted as being very disrespectful to authority in this country.

Over the next several months, the two foreign teachers continue on their separate paths. One teacher getting routine praise, while the other receives increasingly bitter treatment.

For instance, at the end of the first term, all of the teachers and division administrators are gathered for a meeting. The two local directors present awards and high praise for each teacher, except for the foreign teacher they obviously dislike…you.

At this meeting, one of the directors reads aloud several positive comments written for the local teachers and the favored foreign teacher that came from a survey given to parents. The director then reads aloud several negative comments parents wrote about you. Then the director elaborates that the parents were upset with your teaching because the students did very poorly on the English exam that was administered at the end of the term.

The next day, you ask to see the exams but your request is denied. A few days later you discover something shocking. The director, who oversaw all exams, had given your students an exam from a book the students did not use and did not teach from. The other teachers' students were all given exams from the books they used.

Discuss the questions below from your own perspective in small groups of 3-5 members.

1) What would your first reaction be upon discovering that the director gave your students a different exam?

2) Do you think this was an accident?

3) Why do you think the exam from a different book was given to your students?

4) Should you speak to the director about this?

5) Is there an administrator you think you should speak to about this matter?

6) Should the parents be informed that there was a "mistake" with the exams?

7) If you were the foreign principal, how would you handle this matter?

8) As it turns out, you decide to approach the only foreign principal at the school. As you describe what happened, his response is to basically say nothing. Later he makes it clear that there is not much he can do. So, you take the matter up the chain of command, including the local head of the school, and although they seemed sympathetic to your complaints, a few days later you are fired. What do you do next?

9) After being fired, would you feel the battle was worth it?

10) Should the school have a policy regarding any aspect of this situation?

Role-Play Instructions:

A meeting has been called to discuss the issue. Cut out the cards below and place in a stack face down in the center of the table. Each person takes a card at the top of the stack. Read the characteristics of your role, then act accordingly during the meeting. Try to genuinely represent that person's point of view at the meeting. When the meeting has finished, the Observer can provide their feedback and advice on how the meeting transpired and how it might be improved if the meeting were to occur again.

The Objective: Determine what is a fair and balanced resolution to the foreign teacher's complaint.

Foreign Principal	**Local Director 1**
Trained in Western system in New Zealand Lacks leadership skills Married with a family in the country Wants to avoid conflict	Only experience is in local schools Highly nationalistic No training or experience in Western pedagogy or leadership philosophy
Foreign Teacher	**Head of School**
Trained in US Many years of teaching experience Previous management experience Was hired to be foreign principal of the school's new kindergarten next year	Seems sympathetic to your complaints, but says almost nothing during the meeting
Local Director 2	**Observer**
Was the director that read the parents' comments aloud in the meeting Highly nationalistic Will be director of the school's new kindergarten opening next year	Trained professional observer Expert in group dynamics, leadership and conflict resolution Provides feedback and advice at end of meeting

7 Not My Job

Setting the Scene:

Many kindergartens maintain strict control of classroom supplies. In this scenario, the school's policy is that teachers are allowed access to the supply room once per week, and only at designated times when the local manager keeps careful inventory of what each teacher takes.

You are the foreign teacher and manager of the international classrooms. You have worked at the school for three years and are extremely dedicated. The parents absolutely love your teaching style and the kids do too.

One day, you really need to get something from the supply room. The item is very important to the arts and crafts lesson your class will do in 2 hours. The parents will be in attendance because it is part of a special day for parents to spend with their kids at school.

You are standing outside the supply room door. Of course, the door is locked. The local manager will not open the door, stating firmly that supplies can only be accessed during the designated times. That is the rule. You ask the foreign principal, but he does not have a key. The only other person that has a key is the school's accountant. Although he is standing next to the door, he will not open the door either due to the policy. When you ask him why not, he says matter-of-factly, "It's not my job."

Discuss the questions below from your own perspective in small groups of 3-5 members.

1) What is your initial reaction?

2) Can you understand that this culture is very rigid?

3) What would happen if this situation occurred in your country?

4) What do you think is the reason for this policy?

5) If you make a statement against this rigid policy, are you trying to impose your cultural values on another society?

6) Can you think of the exact words to use if you were to explain to the local manager how you disagree with this policy, using the most diplomatic language imaginable?

7) Will this situation affect your attitude about the school and culture?

8) Should you discuss this matter with the owner of the school, whom visits the school several times a week?

9) Isn't this situation the foreign teacher's fault for not being prepared?

10) If you think the school should have a policy regarding this kind of situation, can you write it in one paragraph?

Role-Play Instructions:

A meeting has been called to discuss the issue. Cut out the cards below and place in a stack face down in the center of the table. Each person takes a card at the top of the stack. Read the characteristics of your role, then act accordingly during the meeting. Try to genuinely represent that person's point of view at the meeting. When the meeting has finished, the Observer can provide their feedback and advice on how the meeting transpired and how it might be improved if the meeting were to occur again.

The Objective: Determine what is a fair and balanced resolution to the foreign teacher's complaint.

Foreign Teacher/Manager	**Foreign Principal**
Is both teacher and manager of the international classrooms Extremely dedicated and a very good teacher Parents and kids love this teacher	Favors a more flexible policy in times when needed, like this one Is vocal and expresses his opinion Has no real authority in the school other than over the foreign teachers
Accountant	**Local Principal**
Has no authority to open supply room Is blindly loyal to the owner Will never open that door unless owner says it is okay	Favors traditional practices on all matters Is stern and strict, but has a pleasant demeanor Never compromises
Local Manager	**Observer**
Only experience is in local country Very loyal to local cultural practices Lax management style	Trained professional observer Expert in group dynamics, leadership and conflict resolution Provides feedback and advice at end of meeting

8 Balance-Beam Action Plan

Setting the Scene:

The school has just received a new balance-beam toy for the kindergarten. It is 6 meters long, made of hard plastic, and comes in 4 sections. The top of the beam is about 30 cm. off the floor and sits atop plastic supports on the ends. Apparently, the foreign principal ordered the balance-beam several weeks ago.

The beam is placed on the hardwood floors of the school's large indoor playroom that the students use from 12:30—2:00. There aren't enough toys for the 45 children that don't take naps, nor is there any training offered to teachers or assistants regarding the balance beam. The indoor playroom during naptime is a chaotic mess of young children running wild.

Because the teachers are eating and doing prep work from 12-2, the playroom is supervised by two teaching assistants. The students have no respect for their authority because they know they are just assistants.

You had tried to discuss the unsupervised nature of the indoor playroom with the foreign principal previously, but she was unreceptive. She was actually offended that you would think she needs suggestions and informed you that the school has never had an accident in the playroom, so there is "nothing to worry about."

However, not to be deterred when it comes to student safety, you write a 4-page Action Plan for how to provide adequate supervision of the students in the playroom. Your plan includes a set of structured activities so the kids are not simply left on their own to run around and get out of control. Sadly enough, the foreign principal ridiculed your plan as being too short and lacking detail, even though the school's guidelines for proposals states that 1-3 pages is sufficient.

About six weeks later, one of the students falls off the beam. His elbow smashes onto the hardwood floor and he is rushed to the hospital. He then spends 10 days in the hospital and has 2 metal pins implanted in his elbows.

Discuss the questions below from your own perspective in small groups of 3-5 members.

1) What is your initial reaction to this scenario?

2) What would happen if this situation occurred in your home country?

3) Should the school offer to pay all medical expenses for the student, even ones not covered by insurance?

4) Should you approach the foreign principal again regarding the Action Plan?

5) If the principal again refuses to consider the plan, should the owner of the school be contacted?

6) Should the principal be fired over this incident or should there be any other action taken?

7) If you were the school owner, what would you say to the principal?

8) If you were the parent, what would your reaction be?

9) Should this incident be reported to the government department that oversees kindergarten licensure?

10) Does the school need to formulate a policy regarding a teacher disagreeing with management on a matter that involves student health and safety?

Action Plan Instructions:

Your group is tasked with 2 objectives: 1) examine what should have happened when the school received the balance beam toy and what went wrong, and 2) make an Action Plan for how to handle getting new playground equipment in the future. The Observer can provide feedback at the end of the meeting.

Action Plan: Balance Beam				
Task Goal	Actions to take	Resources needed	Whose Task	Time frame

On the Edge of Their Seats
https://youtu.be/K_BfBOTmtz4
Copy and paste the URL or scan the QR code:

Finger in Face
https://www.youtube.com/watch?v=YCN060Dqf_0
Copy and paste the URL or scan the QR code:

You are the Foreign Principal

9 Hand-foot-and-mouth Disease

Setting the Scene:

Every principal's nightmare involves the school being infected with one of the major childhood diseases. In Southeast Asia, one main childhood disease to be concerned about is Hand-Foot-and-Mouth disease (HFMD), which kills around 100 children each year, usually in June and July. Kindergartens in this region adhere to very strict national guidelines regarding preventing an outbreak. For example, seated at the entrance of a kindergarten is a school nurse. The nurse checks each student's hands and tongue with a special light that helps identify early symptoms of HFMD.

Unfortunately, in this scenario, you are the principal and you have just been informed that a child in one of the K2 classes has been diagnosed with HFMD. Use the discussion questions below to help you design an Action Plan.

Discuss the questions below from your own perspective in small groups of 3-5 members.

1) What are the first 3 steps the school should take at the very moment they learn that a child has been diagnosed as having HFMD?

2) Should the parents of students in other classes be informed?

3) More specifically, how will the K2 students' lunch be handled?

4) Can the kitchen staff contract HFMD by coming in contact with plates and utensils from the K2 class?

5) How will transportation to and from school be handled for the K2 class?

6) One of the K2 students normally takes the bus with students in the K1 class. How will his transportation be handled?

7) What precautions will the teachers in the K2 class need to take?

8) Is it okay for the classes to mix during outdoor free play time?

9) Should the owner of the school be informed?

10) How well do you know the symptoms of the most common childhood diseases?

YouTube Video Supplement

Instructions:

The video on YouTube is a reenactment of this scenario which can be used for a class discussion. The course instructor can play the video in class and guide a class discussion or create several small groups to engage in a discussion. Each group should try to reach a consensus on how the matter should be handled. When each group has formulated a resolution, they can take turns sharing their solution with the class.

HFMD:
https://www.youtube.com/watch?v=XnWiBEAA8II&t=36s
Copy and paste the URL or scan the QR code:

Action Plan Instructions:

Your group is tasked with 2 objectives: 1) examine what should have happened when the school received the balance beam toy and what went wrong, and 2) make an Action Plan for how to handle getting new playground equipment in the future.

Action Plan: HFMD				
Task Goal	Actions to take	Resources needed	Whose Task	Time frame

Research Investigation

Specific Issue Investigated:

Source #1 Key Points	Source #2 Key Points

Summary of Findings:

_____
_____
_____
_____

APA Citation 1:

_____
_____

APA Citation 2:

_____
_____

10 Outdoor Playground Safety Plan

Setting the Scene

There was an incident at a kindergarten on the school's playground that could have been much more serious. The owner of the school decides to hire an outside consulting company to develop a playground safety policy.

So, your consulting firm of education experts has been hired to develop a comprehensive *Playground Safety Plan* for the kindergarten. Your team decides to focus on the outdoor playground first. As a starting point, the kindergarten gives you a diagram of a previous critical incident that occurred. The scenario involves a child rolling down a grassy knoll in a large plastic barrel and almost hitting another student.

As you can see in the playground layout below, the playground is large and wraps around the school building. There are 3 classes at play at the same time and 5 teachers available for duty. The playground is well-equipped with several playhouses, large structures with slides, and plenty of balls, jump-ropes and tricycles.

Using that scenario as a basis:

a) Make a plan that clearly defines what teachers should be doing during the outdoor play period.

b) Make a list of 10 safety rules for students to follow

c) Describe how the outdoor play period is to be stopped each day and students brought back into the building

d) Carefully identify any student actions or behaviors that should heed the teachers' attention urgently

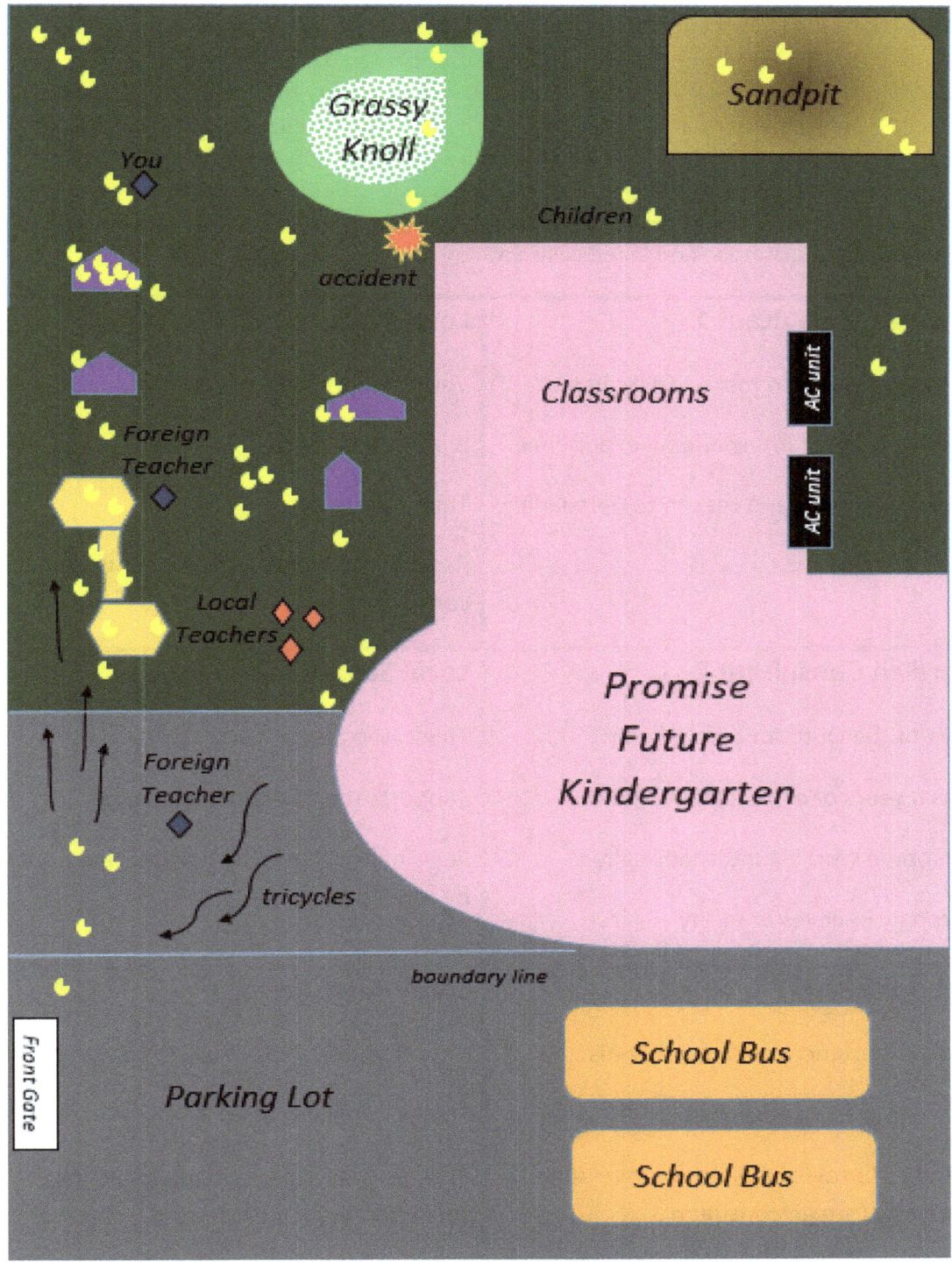

Role-Play Instructions:

Now that your team has finished the plan, it is time to present it to the school's management team. Although the owner has not seen the plan, he has made it clear that getting the management team's approval is extremely important. Unfortunately, from the very beginning, the local principal and VP have been reluctant to cooperate. When you asked for specific information, such as how many accidents have occurred in the last 3 years or what types of injuries are most frequent, you have received zero assistance. From the management team's perspective, the kindergarten is their responsibility and an outside firm is definitely unwelcome.

Foreign Consultant 1	**Local Principal**
Hired by owner to make safety plan	Very traditional local way of thinking
Has 22 years of international experience.	Is stern and strict
Uses diplomacy and reason to persuade others	Thinks the playground is safe
	Resents the owner obtaining outside consultants
Foreign Consultant 2	**Local School V.P.**
Part of the Outdoor Safety Team	Thinks the playground is safe
Has 8 years of experience in the USA	Supports the local principal 100%
First time working internationally	Feels national pride is being threatened by foreigners
Strongly believes in safety	
School Nurse	**Local Head Teacher**
Only experience is in local schools	Very traditional local way of thinking
Very loyal to local ways	Thinks the playground is safe
Refuses to reveal any safety data when asked by foreign consultants	Resents the owner obtaining outside consultants

11 Christmas Show Sabotage

Setting the Scene:
The Christmas show was supposed to be a big event at the kindergarten. The local parents love to see their kids on stage. Most local kindergartens will have 2 big shows a year, plus 3 or 4 more small shows for the parents held in the classrooms every term. This particular Christmas show was being produced by the foreign principal and was to highlight the foreign teachers' efforts.

You met with the foreign teachers 2 months before the show to discuss the general plan: each class will sing one song or do one play, 3-6 minutes long, submit requests for costumes and materials with prices listed, and provide all musical selections to the IT guy as soon as possible.

About 4 weeks before the show, you, the local principal and the VP went to each class to see the first rehearsals. Everything looked pretty good. Of course, some classes were doing better than others. Some songs and movements needed to be made simpler by the teacher. After some adjustments, the next rehearsal two-weeks later looked much better. About 10 days before the show the owner took you on an extended business trip with him to scout out other business opportunities. So, you left everything in the hands of the local principal, who was very experienced and rumored to be the mother of the owner.

You arrive back in town the day before the show. The night before the show the principal told you she was too ill to be the show's MC. That is a bit problem because you don't speak the local language well enough to be the MC, but the VP refused to do it, and all the local managers said they were "too shy." So, you had no choice. One of the secretaries agreed to translate, but during the show there were many times when she just stared at you after you finished speaking a short phrase or sentence. She just said nothing.

The local teachers were supposed to know where to line-up outside of the auditorium to wait their class's turn, but they did not. When you went to provide some directions, they simply did not comply. And then, to your complete surprise, none of the students sang their songs in English. They only danced a little to the music, but sang nothing. Not even the ones that had rehearsed for over a month. Only half of the decorations were up and there was not a single beverage or snack in sight. A few days later you discover that while you were away, the local principal went to each classroom and told the foreign teachers that the students were to NOT sing in English. Why none of the foreign teachers told you this is still a mystery.

The only positive aspect of the show was one traditional song and dance performed by a specially selected group of students that had rehearsed for many weeks with the dance teacher.

As the foreign principal, you were held 100% responsible. Later you discovered that while you were out of town, the local principal went to each classroom and instructed the foreign teachers that the kids were **_not_** to sing in English, at all.

In addition, you spent a considerable amount of time trying to find out why the beverages and snacks were not prepared by the kitchen staff. These arrangements were supposed to have been made by the local principal. She insists she made them, but no one can provide an explanation about why there were no snacks or beverages for the show. Of course, the fact that you cannot speak the local language is a huge disadvantage. Often when you are asking for information, 2 or 3 of the locals in the room will begin to discuss the situation amongst themselves, and despite your repeated instructions for your bilingual secretary to translate, she usually just stands there.

But now the parents are furious. They were told what a good show it was going to be and their expectations were quite high. Now, they are extremely upset and have demanded a meeting with the foreign principal.

You, the local principal and VP meet with approximately 30 of the parents in a large conference room. During the meeting many parents lecture you about the importance of education for their children. They remind you of the school's high tuition. They state, repeatedly, how disappointed they are that the show was so bad, the worst show they have ever seen. Often, the parent will speak loudly and in an angry tone for up to 10 minutes at a time.

You are a bit torn about what to do about this. On the one hand, your job is to protect the school as much as possible, but at the same time, you have learned of the local principal's shenanigans and you feel she should take the blame.

Discuss the questions below from your own perspective in small groups of 3-5 members.

1) What is your initial reaction after reading this scenario?

2) Why do you think the local principal prohibited the students from singing in English?

3) Would you stop the parents during their rant and inform the parents about the local principal sabotaging the show?

4) Can you speculate as to why the foreign teachers did not inform the foreign principal ahead of time that they were told the students should not sing in English?

5) Should you confront the local principal, and if so, what exactly would you say?

6) Should you discuss this matter with the owner, immediately, later, or not at all?

7) Some of the parents are demanding that the foreign principal be fired. Should this happen? Should the parents be told the truth at this point?

8) How will this situation affect the working relations between the foreign and local principal.

9) If you were the owner and you knew about everything that happened and why, how would you handle this matter?

10) How will this situation affect the parents' impressions of the school?

Role-Play Instructions:

Cut out the cards below and place in a stack face down in the center of the table. Each person takes a card at the top of the stack. Read the characteristics of your role, then act accordingly during the meeting. Try to genuinely represent that person's point of view at the meeting. When the meeting has finished, the Observer can provide their feedback and advice on how the meeting transpired and how it might be improved if the meeting were to occur again.

The Objective: Try to come to a consensus regarding how to address the parents' complaints about the Christmas show.

Foreign Principal	**Local Principal**
Knows about the sabotage	Says nothing in your defense
Torn between protecting the school and taking the blame or defending themselves	Sabotaged the show
Doesn't know about the fake parent	Arranged for a fake parent to attend so that they could complain in English
Local Parent 1	**Local Parent 2**
Not really a parent at the school	Highly nationalistic
Lectures the foreign principal, non-stop for 15 minutes	Praises performance of students that sang in the local language
Remarks about how great the kids sang in their own language	Repeatedly remarks about low quality foreign teachers in the country
School VP	**Local Parent 3**
Only experience is in local schools	Favors local practices
Very loyal to local ways	Disappointed with the show
Lax management style	Agrees and nods with others
Never expresses an opinion	Speaks very little English

12 Pocketknife in the Kindy

Setting the Scene:
You have just assumed the position of interim foreign principal of a large kindergarten. The school has 12 foreign teachers from all over the world (England, France, Philippines, India, S. Africa, and the USA). On your second day, one foreign teacher informs you that the American teacher carries a pocketknife to school attached to his belt, and he wears it in the classroom too. Apparently, the previous foreign principal had given the teacher a verbal warning about the knife and clearly instructed him not to wear it. After hearing this news (and getting over the initial shock), you immediately proceed to the teacher's classroom. When you walk into the room you see that the foreign teacher is indeed wearing a small pocketknife on his belt.

Discuss the questions below from your own perspective in small groups of 3-5 members.

1) What are your exact words to the foreign teacher?

2) The law says you cannot fire a teacher without at least 2 prior warnings, one verbal and one written. What now?

3) The foreign teacher wants to know if someone told you about his knife?

4) Should you speak to the previous foreign principal?

5) Should you discuss this matter with the owner, prior to entering the classroom, afterwards, or not at all?

6) Should the parents be informed about this matter?

7) You inform the owner of this matter and he is quite upset. He states that you should have been more observant and is extremely disappointed.

8) Can you think of some legal issues that arise with this scenario?

9) Should the school have a policy regarding any aspect of this situation?

10) Several parents have learned about the teacher carrying the knife and have requested an immediate meeting with you and the owner? Role-play this scenario.

Role-Play Instructions:

Cut out the cards below and place in a stack face down in the center of the table. Each person takes a card from the top of the stack. Read the characteristics of your role, then act accordingly during the meeting. Try to genuinely represent that person's point of view at the meeting. When the meeting has finished, the Observer can provide their feedback and advice on how the meeting transpired and how it might be improved if the meeting were to occur again.

The Objective: Determine if the foreign teacher should be fired and the appropriate procedure to do so.

Foreign Principal	**Local Principal**
Understands severity of the situation, but also knows the foreign teacher may have a mental health issue Appreciates the devotion the teacher consistently shows to the school	Believes the foreign principal is responsible for foreign teachers Has zero concept of fairness Wants the teacher fired immediately
Local Parent 1	**Local Parent 2**
Very upset; Believes most foreign teachers are irresponsible and unprofessional Lectures the foreign principal about safety	Upset and bitter; Makes snide remarks about foreigners and the foreign principal Consistently interrupts the foreign principal
Local Parent 3	**Observer**
Cannot speak English well Continuously nods in agreement with the criticisms by the other parents	Trained professional observer Expert in group dynamics, leadership and conflict resolution Provides feedback after meeting

13 Trampoline Trouble

Setting the Scene:

As the foreign principal you have noticed several issues on the playground that should be addressed. One example concerns the number of students on the trampoline at the same time. Yes, the kindergarten has a trampoline (about 20 sq. meters). It is used daily by all classes. As it is now, there may be as many as 12 kids on the trampoline at the same time. You also notice that the two classroom teachers for each class do not monitor the kids very well at all. There is a lot of pushing and shoving and kids falling down while the teachers usually talk to each other.

Being the proactive principal that you are, you coordinate a meeting with the local principal, vice principal, and two managers to develop a set of 10 playground safety rules. Rule 1 is no more than 5 children on the trampoline at one time.

Two weeks after all the teachers have been trained in the new safety rules, you observe at least 10 kids on the trampoline and while the two local class teachers are talking to each other (for nearly 10 minutes). You approach the teachers but they deny not watching the kids and deny that there were that many kids on the trampoline.

One of the teachers is the same teacher that was constantly shaking her head "no" during the training you did a few weeks ago describing the new playground rules. This is also the same teacher that does not instruct her students to hold the rail as they walk up the stairs or stay on the right side of the stairwell. When you try to approach her to discuss something, she often turns her back and acts like she doesn't hear you.

Finally, when you bring the matter up with the owner, his first response was to warn you that "the local teachers could unite and start a protest outside of the school". That was the first concern he expressed after you finished describing the situation.

Discuss the questions below from your own perspective in small groups of 3-5 members.

1) How will you proceed from here?

2) What could be the reasons for the local teacher's behavior?

3) If you could get the teacher to listen to you with an open mind, what exactly would you say?

4) Should you just drop this matter?

5) Can you think of a plan to resolve this matter?

6) Should the parents be informed about the lax safety environment of the school?

7) What will you do the next time you see the teachers allowing 12 kids on the trampoline?

8) One evening while at a local pub, you meet a foreign parent with 2 children that will be moving
to the area in a few months. He asks if you know of a good kindergarten for his kids. What do you say?

9) At an upcoming open house event for foreign parents, one of the moms asks you, specifically,
about the school's safety environment. What do you say?

10) Should the school have a policy regarding any aspect of this situation?

YouTube Video Supplement

Instructions

There are several videos on YouTube that provide short explanations of different scenarios. Each video describes what happens and contains follow-up discussion questions or small-group activities. The course instructor can play the video in the classroom and start a class discussion, or create several small groups to engage in a discussion and try to reach a consensus on how the matter should be handled. When each group has formulated a resolution, they can take turns sharing with the class.

Trampoline Trouble:
https://www.youtube.com/watch?v=jHnZkljN2o0&t=5s
Copy and paste the URL or scan the QR code:

Role Play Instructions:

Cut out the cards below and place in a stack face down in the center of the table. Each person takes a card from the top of the stack. Read the characteristics of your role, then act accordingly during the meeting. Try to genuinely represent that person's point of view at the meeting. When the meeting has finished, the Observer can provide their feedback and advice on how the meeting transpired and how it might be improved if the meeting were to occur again.

The Objective: Satisfy the foreign principal's concerns and determine what, if any, action or policy should be devised.

Foreign Principal Feels frustrated and offended that local teachers refuse to follow the safety rules Thinks the teacher that refused to look at him/her when being spoken to should be reprimanded Is persistent and determined to make local teachers respect his/her authority as principal	**School Owner** Is an accountant by profession and mostly concerned about the school's reputation Number 1 priority is to make money Talks nearly non-stop during meeting Completely avoids the issue of local teachers being rude to the foreign principal
Local Principal Sits attentively and listens to the school owner Takes notes as the owner speaks Fully supports local teachers Does not think the foreign principal should have authority over local teachers	**Local School V.P.** Follows the direction of the owner 100% Nods in agreement consistently as he speaks Only comments involve restating the points made by the owner
Local Manager 1 Barely expresses an opinion in any meeting Nods in agreement with statements from owner, local principal and V.P.	**Observer** Trained professional observer Expert in group dynamics, leadership and conflict resolution Provides feedback and advice at end of meeting

14 Double Trouble

Setting the Scene:

One of the foreign teachers was playing with a child on the trampoline. The teacher was kneeling down and tried to gently flip the student over his shoulder. Unfortunately, at the same time, one of the other kids accidently bounced in the wrong direction. The two kids smashed into each other and the boy being gently flipped had to be sent to the emergency room and suffered a broken nose. Although the break was not severe, the parents are outraged.

The backstory to this event is that this is the second student sent to the hospital while in the care and supervision of this particular foreign teacher. The first time was also an accident and took place in the classroom. Although he is not a good teacher, these events were deemed truly accidental by administrators. This is also the same foreign teacher that was carrying a pocket-knife to the classroom.

Regarding the foreign teacher, although obviously not suited for a classroom position with young children, he has been very devoted to the school for more than 3 years. Whenever the government requires the school to send a teacher to an event, this teacher always volunteers. He is also a devoted member of the local Christian Church and holds the position of secretary. He is incredibly intelligent and always tries to be helpful and supportive of new teachers.

Discuss the questions below from your own perspective in small groups of 3-5 members.

1) If you were the foreign principal, how would you proceed from here?

2) Should a teacher be fired for accidents?

3) This kind of play between adult male and boy is common, but in this southeastern culture it is not. The local teachers and principal cannot accept it. They are so fearful of accidents.

4) If the local principal insists on firing the teacher, how will you handle it?

5) Should you discuss this matter with the owner, immediately, later, or not at all?

6) The parents are demanding that the teacher be fired immediately. Will you comply?

7) The parent of the child with the broken nose has demanded her money be returned.

Unfortunately, she does not have the receipt and the owner refuses to refund her money without it. How will you explain this to the parent (state your exact words)

8) Can you think of some legal issues that arise with this scenario?

9) Several parents are fed-up and are demanding their tuition returned immediately and they have their receipts. How will you respond?

10) What exact words would you use if this teacher walked into your office and asked for a letter of
recommendation?

15 Termination Letter

Setting the Scene:

After various other incidents with students and co-teachers, the school carried out all the necessary steps required by law, and has now decided to terminate the foreign teacher's contract. According to procedure and law, the school must write a termination letter and have a meeting with the employee to clearly explain the reasons for termination.

In addition, all foreign teachers' contracts have a required one-month termination notice. Either the school provides a 30-day notice, or if not, then the school must pay the teacher one month's salary, unless the teacher has violated the morality clause of the contract or has broken the law.

Discuss the questions below from your own perspective in small groups of 3-5 members.

1) Briefly, what should be the main content of this termination letter?

2) In this case, should all the reasons be listed or described in detail?

3) Are there government requirements regarding 3 notices applicable if there is a morality clause in
the contract?

4) Should the school's lawyer be contacted for advice?

5) Should you discuss this matter with the owner, immediately, later, or not at all?

6) How do you think breaking the teacher's contract will affect the attitude of other foreign teachers?

7) How will you start the meeting for firing?

8) What specific words will you use to say "you're fired"?

9) The local principal wants you to be forceful and stern with the teacher at the meeting. How will you respond to this expectation?

10) When another kindergarten calls you to ask about this teacher, what will you say?

Role Play Instructions:

Cut out the cards below and place in a stack face down in the center of the table. Each person takes a card from the top of the stack. Read the characteristics of your role, then act accordingly during the meeting. Try to genuinely represent that person's point of view at the meeting. When the meeting has finished, the Observer can provide their feedback and advice on how the meeting transpired and how it might be improved if the meeting were to occur again.

The Objective: Write a termination letter that satisfies the perspectives of each administrator.

Foreign Principal	**Local Principal**
Agrees contract should be terminated	Has a vey punitive philosophy
Thinks termination letter should have a neutral and professional tone	Wants letter to detail reasons for termination
Would like to offer the teacher a recommendation letter for a non-kindergarten position	Is adamant that no rec. letter should have the school's stamp on it
Local School V.P.	**Local Manager 1**
Supports the local principal in all matters	Barely ever expresses an opinion in any meeting
Is highly nationalistic and has deep resentment towards foreign teachers	Nods in agreement with statements from local principal and V.P.
Local Manager 2	**Observer**
Agrees with the local principal 100 percent	Trained professional observer
Expresses her opinion by restating the local principal's point of view, almost verbatim	Expert in group dynamics, leadership and conflict resolution
	Provides feedback and advice at end of meeting

Four Against One
https://www.youtube.com/watch?v=d4TDEIPN4lI
Copy and paste the URL or scan the QR code:

Applicant Requirements
https://www.youtube.com/watch?v=hHaG3U9L9TY
Copy and paste the URL or scan the QR code:

Division of Labor
https://www.youtube.com/watch?v=iuta_k6rcEE
Copy and paste the URL or scan the QR code:

On the Spot

HOW TO PLAY

On-the-Spot Card Game:
This is a fast-paced card game that involves each player giving their opinion on how to handle a specific scenario. First, form small groups of 3-5 players. Cut out the cards on one of the pages and place them in a stack in the center of the group. One player then picks the top card and reads aloud the scenario described. Then that player says how they would respond and what they would say in that situation. Afterwards, the other members of the group share their opinions on the player's response and how they would handle it.

A slightly different version of this game involves the group discussing the scenario and then arriving at a consensus on what to say and do. It is important to be as specific as possible. So, instead of saying something in general, try to write down the specific words that your group thinks should be used in that scenario. Finally, each group can share their solution with the class and the course instructor can guide a class discussion.

Note: One aspect of conflict resolution is knowing when the situation is serious and when it is best to just "let it go." Not all of the scenarios described on the cards are extremely serious. So, the students must determine when the situation merits confrontation, or diplomacy, or just seeing the matter as frivolous and not worth a long and possibly heated discussion.

Every day at lunch you see that the kids eat with their mouths open. You are not sure if you should try to correct this or not. On one hand, it looks disgusting. On the other hand, this is a cultural difference. One day your co-teacher notices you looking oddly at the children during lunch and she asks, "Is everything okay?"	Near the end of the day, you remember that you have to finish cleaning up in the art room. You go to the teacher's office first and discover that your co-teacher has placed several paint pallets on your desk and says, "you forgot to clean them." She was the one that actually poured too much paint into the pallets and did not help at all with the clean-up.
This is your first job in this foreign country. After 3 weeks there is national holiday on a Wednesday and Thursday. The school informs the teachers that according to the law in ____, everyone will get the holidays off but will be required to work the following Saturday and Sunday. There is no change in salary.	After 28 hours in 4 planes, you take a bus, wait for the school's van (which was late), and travel another 45 minutes to the school. All you really want to do is take a shower. However, you're told that you must go to the training session that has already started. As soon as you enter the room, the school director walks up to you and says, "you're late."
As the foreign director of a new Australian kindergarten, you have been told that the class size will be no larger than 20. When discussing this with the local principal, she says the classrooms can fit at least 24. You remind her of the Australian owner's instructions. She looks at you squarely in the eyes and says, "this is ____. The class size will be 24."	You are the foreign principal of a new school. After catching your secretary lying to you multiple times, you decide to fire her. You tell the owner that you would like to choose your next secretary. Six weeks later the owner comes to your office and introduces your new secretary, whom you have never met.

You notice a lot of potentially dangerous practices on the playground. You approach the local director and offer to make a playground safety handbook. The director says they have one already. So, you ask to see it. She says it is in the local language so you would not understand it. You reply that it is okay because you can have a friend translate the key parts….no problem; you are curious about the rules. After a few weeks go by, you ask again and she says she is busy at that moment. A few more weeks go by and she still has not given you a copy.

Every day the local principal posts photos of the students' lunch on the school's website. You notice that several times a week the photos don't actually match what the kids are served. There are some items in the photos that the kids don't get at all. During a parent/teacher meeting, one of the parents makes a comment to you and your co-teacher about how delicious the meals look each day. The co-teacher nods proudly and says that the school takes nutrition very seriously. The parent then looks directly at you.

It is your third day. You need to go to the Foreign Affairs office for paperwork but you can't find the office. You ask some staff in other offices but they can't speak English and your ability to speak the local language is horrendous. After 45 minutes you return to the classroom and ask your co-teacher for help. She takes you directly to the office and says sarcastically "there it is…easy to find". But when you look at the office sign it says "Library Office." As it turns out, the offices were moved over the summer but no one changed the signs.

You are the co-teacher of a K2 class in the international division of a kindergarten. You were educated and trained in the West and have worked in several countries for over 12 years. Your co-teacher has 5 years of experience in a local school and has never been outside of the country. On the first day of class, the local director announces that the local teacher is the lead teacher in the classroom, she will coordinate the daily schedule and is "in charge" of classroom-related issues.

You agreed to teach extra classes for extra pay under the condition that you teach the way you want. After 2 months, the director says that you cannot use coloring pages. You explain that the coloring pages match the lesson's theme and that you go to pairs of students and ask them questions such as "what are you doing?" You then teach them how to answer with proper pronunciation, starting with, "coloring" and over several weeks incrementally working up to "I am coloring the bird pink and purple." You think it is a great way to focus on pronunciation and teach practical language skills. The director has never seen the lesson, but says that coloring pages are prohibited.

You are asked to teach about inventions with just a few moments notice because your co-teacher needs to go to the HR office for some reason. One invention you are supposed to cover is the "telescope." You don't have a flashcard, but just then, the local principal steps into the room. So, you ask if she could say the name for "telescope" in the local language. She says there is no need because the students know the word in English. You explain that maybe some do, but not all; you just want to make sure they all understand. The principal reiterates that all the students know the word in English and says sternly, "we speak English in _____."

You are the foreign principal of an old kindergarten. You were hired by the owner to make some new "international" style classrooms. You ask one of the local managers if they know of a local builder so you can consult with them about the costs of making modifications to one of the classrooms. The manager refuses to help because she "will not let you destroy the school."

You are teaching part-time in a public school on a 3-month contract starting in January. One day, it's -5°C outside. When you walk into the classroom you notice that all 34 students are wearing their winter coats, gloves, and hats. Then you notice that all of the windows are open. You are sure that you will catch the flu if you teach in that environment. You notice that in all of the classrooms the windows are wide open.

The contract you signed is to be the foreign principal of a large kindergarten with nearly 600 students. After a few weeks on the job the owner tells you he is going to open an education center for babies in a different part of town. He asks you to design the curriculum, the interior layout and furnishings, as well as the teacher-training program. He thinks you should do this work because you now work for his company. He offers no additional salary or compensation.

After 3 months of a 1-year contract it is clear that the local teachers and staff will not follow your very politely delivered directions. You are beginning to understand why you are the 7th foreign principal in less than 5 years. You discuss the matter with the owner and he reassures you that things will change. You decide to keep a record over the next month. Six weeks later, 15 out of the 22 tasks you requested from the local teachers and staff were still not completed. What can you do?

You are at a meeting with the local management team. You notice that the principal has a tube of instant coffee. This strikes you as odd because you know she does not drink coffee. At the end of the meeting, she asks to speak to you privately as one of the local managers translates. The principal then uses the instant coffee tube as a color guide. She points to the lighter shades of brown as an acceptable skin color for teachers that you hire in the future. She indicates that darker shades are not acceptable for hiring.

The local teacher you work with has Montessori certification and has worked in the same classroom with the same students for 18 months. During a parent-teacher meeting a parent complains that the toys and materials have been the same the whole time her child has been in that classroom (18 months). Your co-teacher tells the parent that the school plans to buy more materials in the next few months, but you know this is not true. The parent then looks directly at you and seems suspicious.

You are the foreign principal of a soon to open Australian kindergarten in an Asian country. At your first meeting with the local consultant, which the Australian company was required to hire, she begins by speaking very loudly, telling you how the school will be managed, what the key features will be, and your limited role. She talks nonstop for over 10 minutes and at one point bangs her fist on the table. You look at your secretary who is translating, sometimes, and you ask how much longer you have to put up with this. Your secretary says you must listen because the consultant is famous and well-respected in _____.	The kindergarten is having a Saturday picnic; everyone is to meet on campus at 9:30 a.m. Two foreign teachers call the local manager because they can't get a taxi to understand their directions. She arranges a taxi but the bus leaves promptly at 9:30. Less than a minute later the teachers call you (the foreign principal); they just arrived on campus. You ask the local manager to tell the driver to turn around and pick them up. She replies that she will not because it is the teachers' fault for being late. You instruct the bus driver to return to campus, but he refuses. It is clear that you have no authority, not even over the bus driver.
After working in this country for several years, you have learned that local teachers have to follow a much stricter set of rules than foreign teachers. In the interest of treating everyone equally, you conduct a training session that describes various policy changes meant to treat all teachers the same. However, it becomes evident that the local staff do not want the new policies. They think you are trying to impose Western values on their culture and this threatens their sense of nationalism. What should you do?	You are the foreign director of an Australian kindergarten in _____ that will open in 2 months. The Australian corporation is very clear about adhering to local regulations while also including key features of Australian schools. You are having a meeting with the local principal to set the lunch menu that is supposed to be a combination of Eastern and Western food. The local principal states that "this is _____" so the menu will be _____." She finishes by saying that you should concern yourself with the English program and that is it.

Part of your job is to observe the foreign teachers doing 30-minute teaching demos and then provide feedback to each teacher individually. You try to be as encouraging as possible, highlighting the positives and offering suggestions for improvement. But yet there are two foreign teachers from a very poor country where English is not the native language. In the one-on-one meeting one of them says that their country has a great education system and their English is better than American teachers.	After 2 weeks into a new position as foreign principal, one of the foreign teachers tells you that he had drinks with the owner a few nights ago. This is common in _____. The teacher informs you that the owner told him that you have a drinking problem and are divorced with 3 kids in your home country that you don't support (none of which is true). You are not surprised because he often makes disparaging comments to you about current and previous employees. How would you handle this matter?
Every day at lunch the kids in your class like to talk to each other. But your co-teacher keeps telling them to be quiet and eat.	You are a male teacher in a kindergarten. You have just started and several times during your first month, you notice the female principal peeking around the corner from inside the children's bathroom that is attached to the classroom. She seems to be spying on you.

You are telling a local teacher that the Australian company that owns school want the classrooms to be bright and vivid, instead of the usual pastel pinks and blues so common in that country. Your secretary is supposed to translate your instructions but refuses because she disagrees. You state that the secretary is to translate, not approve or disapprove decisions. She then says she is on the BoD and can override you. She was hired as a secretary, but because that nation's law requires 5 local citizens be on the BoD, you know that she was asked to sign that paper as a formality only.	The school has a parallel management structure: one for foreign teachers, one for local teachers. Foreign teachers often complain about their co-teachers being difficult and uncooperative. When you express those concerns to the local principal, she refuses to even discuss the matter and says it is just a "misunderstanding." This has created a very unpleasant environment. It is difficult for you to keep good foreign teachers because they get frustrated and leave when their contract is completed. You have indeed lost some very good teachers, but you are responsible for ensuring the quality of instruction.
Like every school in _____, foreign teachers get paid 4 or 5 times the salary of local teachers, receive better health-care and get paid vacations. Local teachers have more responsibilities, spend more time working after hours and face harsh penalties if parents complain or the school loses students. Understandably, the local teachers resent this imbalance and sometimes their frustration can be seen when interacting with their foreign co-teachers. The owner refuses to change anything.	The school's owner has tasked you to redesign the library. So, you approach the librarian and as nicely as you can, ask for her input. Your secretary translates. You want to move some shelves to a different side of the room, but the librarian says the owner told her that could not be done. She finds a reason to reject every suggestion. Later, during a meeting with the owner you describe the librarian's attitude. He is reluctant to believe it. So, you ask your secretary to confirm what you are describing. She sits in silence; says absolutely nothing each time you ask.

An Australian company has hired you to open a kindergarten in _____. You are the third foreign director in 8 months and have no idea why the others left. To be a team player, you agreed to teach for 2 hours in the mornings because good foreign teachers are hard to find. Unfortunately, the local director has decided to hold all meetings while you are teaching, so you are completely left out of decision-making. You discuss this with her and explain that you need to be at meetings. She says "okay" but then keeps scheduling the meetings when you are in the classroom.	The school has devised a playground safety handbook. The local management team and you, the foreign principal, worked on it together. As you are presenting the rules to all of the teachers, there are 2 local teachers sitting in the front row that keep shaking their heads. You ask if they have any questions, but they give no response. You are sure they understand English and the PowerPoint is in both English and the local language. This behavior continues throughout the training. What do you do?
After you fired your secretary for repeatedly lying to you and not doing as you asked, the owners promote her to manage 2 of their language centers. You work in the same office and now she refuses to speak to you and turns her head when passing by. You bring the issue up with the owners and let them know your thoughts on professionalism. They are not concerned. A month later you are assigned to attend the Halloween party at the location furthest from your home, while the secretary you fired is assigned to the location closest to you.	You have been assigned to teach English lessons to the students each day for 30 minutes. It is a fun lesson and you enjoy teaching the enthusiastic children. One day the kids are speaking a lot to each other in their native language, so you instruct them to try to speak to each other in English during English class. At that point your co-teacher, who is sitting nearby at her desk, says sternly, "They're _____ so they speak _____. This isn't America".

APPENDIX A: SELF-REFLECTION WORKSHEET

Instructions: Take a few moments to think about the role play activity or action plan you just completed. Consider your actions and how others responded. Now, using the 5-point scale below, indicate the degree to which you agree or disagree with the statement on the left.

1=totally disagree   2=somewhat disagree   3=neither agree/disagree
4=somewhat agree   5=totally agree

Reflection Statements:	1	2	3	4	5	Adjectives: List adjectives that describe your feelings related to this statement.
I learned something about group dynamics.						
I am happy with how I interacted with others.						
I developed insight into how culture affects behavior.						
I learned a little bit about myself during this activity.						
I participated in this activity in a professional manner.						
Our group handled the activity well.						

There was considerable conflict in our group.					
Decisions were made objectively and without bias.					
All group members contributed equally.					
My opinions were respected by others in the group.					
Discussions often got off-track.					
Our group showed harmony and collective decision-making.					
Group members listened to each other's opinion.					
One member tried to dominate the discussion.					
Overall, I am satisfied with my experience.					

APPENDIX B: SETTING NEW GOALS WORKSHEET

Instructions: Think about the aspects of your actions during this activity you would like to improve. Use the 5-point scale below to indicate how important each area of improvement is to you by placing a check-mark in the appropriate column. Then, describe what you plan to do next time to improve in each area.

1=not important at all 2=somewhat unimportant 3=slightly important 4=somewhat important 5=extremely important

Area of Improvement:	1	2	3	4	5	Set New Goals: Write in specific terms
Be more task-focused.						
Handle conflict more professionally.						
Encourage others to participate.						
Show more interest in the discussion.						
Be more open-minded to others' suggestions.						
Be a better listener.						
Be more assertive to get my point across.						
Stand firm when others disagree with my point of view/suggestions.						
Step-in and try to reduce conflict among other group members.						
Try to point-out areas of agreement.						
Be less critical of others' suggestions.						
Communicate my perspective more clearly and concisely.						
Talk less so that others have more opportunity to express their views.						

APPENDIX C: OBSERVER FORM

Descriptor Statement	Totally Disagree 1	Disagree 2	Unsure 3	Agree 4	Totally Agree 5
Everyone participated in the discussion.	○	○	○	○	○
Everyone's opinion was heard and respected.	○	○	○	○	○
Communication was not always open and honest.	○	○	○	○	○
The tone of the discussion was professional at all times.	○	○	○	○	○
The group stayed on task.	○	○	○	○	○
Disagreements were handled with hostility.	○	○	○	○	○
All participants took the task seriously.	○	○	○	○	○
The group often became distracted with minor issues.	○	○	○	○	○
The meeting was productive.	○	○	○	○	○
Some members attempted to block progress.	○	○	○	○	○

ABOUT THE AUTHOR

Dr. Cornell has worked in the field of education for 30 years. His work includes university teaching, training kindergarten and primary school teachers in 8 countries, working as a kindergarten classroom teacher, and serving as a start-up consultant for 8 baby centers and kindergartens in 3 countries. He has designed 3 education programs: The Sunflower Baby cognitive development program for infants, the Baby-Brain English program for ages 6 mos. – 2 years, and the Tea-Time EFL program for ages 2-6 years old. His current book, *Cross-Cultural ECE,* is based on 12 years of experience working in foreign countries, primarily in Southeast Asia.